INTEGRATING YOU

A Groundbreaking Approach to Wholeness Through Somatic Internal Family Systems Therapy

Healing Trauma through Somatic IFS with Real-World Applications and Case Studies

Rosie Peggy Greenwood

Contents

Author's Note

Dear Reader,

Thank you for journeying with me through the pages of this book, "Integrating You: A Groundbreaking Approach to Wholeness Through Somatic Internal Family Systems Therapy". It has been a deep honor and a privilege to share these insights and discoveries with you.

From my own journey as a researcher, I understand the transformative potential of therapies like Internal Family Systems (IFS) and Somatic Therapy. The fusion of these two modalities into Somatic IFS opens up a new dimension of understanding and healing, and I hope this book has offered a comprehensive exploration of this innovative approach.

My goal has always been to make the principles and practices of Somatic IFS accessible, practical, and empowering. Whether you are a professional seeking to broaden your therapeutic toolkit, or an individual looking to understand and heal yourself better, I hope this book has served you well.

Remember, the journey towards wholeness isn't always linear or straightforward. It involves patience, courage, and compassion. As you continue on your path, remember to honor your unique rhythm, to respect each of your parts, and above all, to lead with your true Self.

This book is just a starting point, a guide to a vast landscape of self-discovery and growth. I encourage you to continue exploring, learning, and evolving. Each of us has the capacity for incredible change and growth, and I am excited for you to uncover your own potential.

Finally, I extend my deepest gratitude to all the pioneers in the fields of IFS and Somatic Therapy, whose wisdom and insights form the bedrock of this work. Their tireless pursuit of understanding and healing continues to inspire and guide us all.

Thank you once again for being a part of this journey. Here's to your continued growth, self-discovery, and the journey towards wholeness.

With deepest respect,

Chapter 1: Foundations of Internal Family Systems Therapy

Understanding the Self

In the Internal Family Systems model, the Self is the centerpiece, the core essence of an individual. It's a concept that encompasses much more than merely an amalgamation of different parts or an overarching sense of personal identity.

What is the Self?

The Self, according to IFS, is your true, authentic, undamaged essence. It's the seat of consciousness, the 'I' in 'I am'. It is not a part or a collection of parts but rather the entity that possesses the ability to understand, empathize with, and heal the parts.

The Self is inherently positive, containing qualities of compassion, curiosity, calmness, confidence, creativity, courage, clarity, and connectedness - often referred to as the '8 Cs' in IFS. The Self is that part of us that can listen without judgment, that can hold space for our emotions, and that can make balanced, wise decisions.

The Role of the Self in IFS

In the IFS model, the goal is to enable the Self to assume its natural leadership role within our internal system. This isn't about fighting or suppressing our parts; instead, it's about creating a space where every part is heard and valued, under the gentle and compassionate leadership of the Self.

The Self, when in a leadership role, can navigate the complexities of our internal world, enabling healing and integration. It can approach each part with curiosity, striving to understand its perspective and its positive intent. It can provide comfort to exiled parts, negotiate with managers, and calm firefighters, fostering a sense of harmony and cooperation among all parts.

Uncovering the Self

Unfortunately, the Self often gets obscured by our parts, especially when they take over or blend with us. Stress, trauma, societal pressures, and other life experiences can cause our parts to act out, causing us to lose touch with our Self.

The therapeutic journey in IFS involves helping individuals unblend from their parts and access their Self. This process often begins with simple mindfulness exercises, such as focusing on the breath or bodily sensations, to create some distance from our parts.

The more we can access and embody our Self, the more we can understand and heal our parts. This leads to a greater sense of internal harmony, personal growth, and overall wellbeing.

The Power of the Self

Understanding and accessing the Self can be transformative. When we're in Self, we feel more balanced, centered, and whole. We're able to relate to others with more empathy and kindness, and we're better equipped to handle life's challenges with grace and resilience.

In essence, the Self is not something we need to develop or cultivate; it's always there, waiting to be uncovered and allowed to lead. By accessing our Self, we can start the journey towards healing and integration, embodying a more authentic and vibrant version of ourselves.

Parts in IFS

The concept of 'parts' is one of the most innovative and powerful aspects of Internal Family Systems Therapy (IFS). Let's explore this concept in more detail.

What Are Parts?

In the IFS model, 'parts' are sub-personalities or facets of our psyche that have their own distinct feelings, thoughts, roles, and viewpoints. Each of us has multiple parts, and no part is inherently bad or wrong. All parts have valuable qualities and, even if they're causing problems, they're doing so out of an attempt to be helpful.

Richard Schwartz, the creator of IFS, believes that these parts aren't just metaphors or symbolic representations; they're actual, discrete entities within our minds. Our parts can take over or blend with us, leading us to act or feel in particular ways that might seem out of character or even contrary to our actual desires or values.

Types of Parts

In IFS, parts are broadly classified into three types: exiles, managers, and firefighters. Each type has a distinct role in our internal system and contributes to our overall mental and emotional health.

Exiles are parts that hold the memories and emotions from traumatic experiences or difficult life events. To protect us from the pain, these parts are often exiled or pushed away from our conscious awareness. They carry burdens of extreme beliefs, emotions, and sensations. These parts may feel stuck in the past and can get triggered by situations that remind them of the original trauma.

Managers are the parts that strive to maintain control of our inner and outer environments. They try to prevent the exiles' pain from surfacing by keeping us focused on day-to-day tasks and responsibilities. Managers can show up as critical parts, perfectionist parts, caretaking parts, or people-pleasing parts. While their methods can be problematic, their intention is to protect us.

Firefighters spring into action when the exiles' pain becomes too intense and starts to seep into our consciousness. They use distracting behaviors, such as addiction, self-harm, binge-eating, or rage, to numb the pain and divert our attention from the distressing emotions or memories. Like managers, firefighters aim to protect us, even if their actions might seem harmful or extreme.

Working With Parts in Therapy

The ultimate goal of IFS therapy is to foster a harmonious relationship between the Self (our core, authentic self) and the various parts. This process involves recognizing and acknowledging our parts, understanding their roles and intentions, helping them release their burdens, and integrating them into our internal family system in a healthy way.

The first step is to build awareness of our parts and approach them with curiosity, compassion, and non-judgment. This shift in perspective can be transformative, enabling us to view our behaviors, emotions, and thoughts with greater empathy and understanding.

Next, we strive to unburden our parts, which involves healing the exiles and helping the managers and firefighters adopt healthier strategies. This process often involves revisiting painful memories or experiences in a safe and supportive environment.

Finally, once the parts have released their burdens, they can shift from their extreme roles to more balanced and beneficial roles. As this internal transformation takes place, individuals often report feeling more integrated, resilient, and whole.

Let's take a closer look at the concept of 'parts' within Internal Family Systems (IFS) therapy with some practical examples:

1. Exiles:

Imagine a child who was constantly criticized by their parents. This child might develop an exiled part that carries feelings of worthlessness and rejection. This part may resurface when the individual faces criticism as an adult, overwhelming them with those same childhood feelings.

Example: Jack, a high-performing executive, feels a deep sense of worthlessness whenever his boss points out minor mistakes in his work. He is not usually affected by such criticisms, but in these moments, he feels the same crushing sense of rejection that he did as a child when his parents were overly critical of him. Here, the feelings of worthlessness belong to an exiled part that carries the pain of his past.

2. Managers:

A manager part might develop to protect the individual from the pain carried by the exiles. It might do this by driving the person to excel in everything, thus avoiding any potential criticism.

Example: In Jack's case, he might have a manager part that pushes him to work tirelessly. It ensures that he double-checks all his reports and stays late at the office to finish his work. This part aims to shield him from the criticism that might awaken his exiled part.

3. Firefighters:

If for some reason, a criticism gets through, a firefighter part might jump in to distract Jack from the exiled part's pain.

Example: When Jack's boss points out a minor mistake, his firefighter part might react by making him binge eat junk food to numb the pain and distract him from the feelings of worthlessness that his exiled part is bringing up.

These parts may manifest differently in different people. The manager part might make someone a perfectionist, or it could cause them to procrastinate to avoid potential failure. A firefighter part might cause one person to overeat, another person to drink excessively, and another person to launch into anger.

The goal of IFS is not to eliminate these parts but to help them find healthier roles within your internal system. As therapy progresses, Jack might learn to relate to his parts with compassion, understanding their protective intentions. This could help his manager part trust that it doesn't need to push him so hard, and his firefighter part learn other ways to soothe his pain. His exiled part could then express its pain and heal, reducing the extreme reactions of the other parts. In the end, Jack would feel more integrated and less at war with himself.

The concept of parts in IFS offers a unique and compassionate framework for understanding and transforming our internal world. By recognizing and honoring all parts of ourselves, we can cultivate inner harmony and foster deep, lasting healing.

The IFS Therapy Process

The Internal Family Systems (IFS) therapy process is a transformative journey, which involves building a relationship between the Self and the various parts. It's an empowering, client-led process that respects each person's unique experiences and pacing. Let's delve deeper into the three primary stages of this process: Accessing, Unburdening, and Integration.

1. Accessing

The initial phase in the IFS therapeutic process is Accessing. This stage focuses on building awareness of the different parts, identifying their roles, and starting to develop relationships with them.

Therapists may use various techniques, such as meditation or guided imagery, to help clients connect with their parts. Clients are encouraged to approach their parts with curiosity, openness, and non-judgment, even when the parts seem destructive or problematic.

For example, a client might initially feel hostile towards a part that provokes feelings of anxiety. However, as the client starts to access and understand this part, they might realize that it's trying to protect them from potential dangers or disappointments. This understanding can foster empathy towards the part, paving the way for healing and transformation.

2. Unburdening

Once a part has been accessed and understood, the next step is Unburdening. This process involves releasing the extreme beliefs, emotions, and sensations ('burdens') that the parts carry, particularly the exiles.

Unburdening is a delicate, gradual process that requires a lot of care and patience. The therapist creates a safe and supportive space for the client to revisit painful memories or experiences, which the exiles are often stuck in. The client, led by the Self, can then help the part let go of its burdens, heal from past traumas, and shift towards a healthier role.

3. Integration

Following the unburdening process, the parts are ready to change their roles and integrate into the internal system healthily. Integration doesn't mean eliminating or merging the parts; instead, it refers to a harmonious co-existence where all parts are valued and heard.

As the parts let go of their burdens and extreme roles, they often discover new, beneficial roles within the system. For instance, a part that used to provoke anxiety to keep the person safe might transform into a part that encourages careful planning and preparedness. Similarly, a part that used to trigger self-harming behaviors to distract from pain might evolve into a part that promotes self-care and stress relief.

The integration stage is characterized by a sense of internal harmony, resilience, and wholeness. Clients often report feeling more in touch with their true Self and more compassionate towards all parts of themselves.

The IFS therapy process is not a linear one. These stages can overlap, and a client may cycle through them multiple times as they work with different parts. Yet, regardless of the specific path, the goal remains the same: to empower the Self, heal the parts, and foster a sense of internal harmony and wholeness. This groundbreaking approach holds the potential for profound personal growth and lasting transformation.

The Power of IFS

Internal Family Systems (IFS) therapy stands out for its empathetic and empowering approach to healing. It views the mind as a complex ecosystem of parts, each with its valuable contribution. By fostering a harmonious relationship between these parts and the Self, IFS promotes deep, lasting healing. Let's explore the various ways that IFS demonstrates its transformative power:

1. Empathy and Non-Judgment

IFS encourages us to approach every part with curiosity, compassion, and non-judgment. This perspective can be incredibly healing, allowing us to view our behaviors, thoughts, and feelings with greater understanding and empathy.

For example, a person struggling with addiction might have a firefighter part that's trying to numb the pain of an exiled part. Instead of viewing the addiction as a weakness or failing, IFS sees it as an extreme attempt to protect the individual from pain. This shift in perspective can reduce feelings of shame and guilt, fostering a more compassionate and healing relationship with oneself.

2. Empowerment and Self-Leadership

IFS places the individual—not the therapist—in the driver's seat. The therapy process empowers individuals to lead their healing journey, guided by the wisdom of their Self. This approach can lead to profound self-discovery and personal growth, enhancing feelings of autonomy and resilience.

3. Healing Trauma

IFS is particularly effective in addressing trauma. The therapy process helps individuals access, unburden, and heal exiled parts that carry traumatic memories or emotions. This approach can alleviate symptoms of post-traumatic stress disorder (PTSD) and other trauma-related conditions, fostering emotional regulation and recovery.

4. Systemic Perspective

IFS views the mind as an ecosystem of interacting parts, much like a family. This systemic perspective enables a holistic approach to healing, addressing the underlying dynamics and relationships between parts rather than just focusing on symptomatic relief.

5. Lasting Change

By addressing the root causes of emotional distress and fostering internal harmony, IFS promotes lasting change. As parts release their burdens and adopt healthier roles, individuals often experience significant improvements in their mental health, relationships, and overall quality of life.

6. Broad Applicability

IFS has been applied successfully in various therapeutic contexts, including individual therapy, couples therapy, family therapy, and group therapy. It's also been used to address a wide range of mental health conditions, including anxiety disorders, mood disorders, personality disorders, eating disorders, and addiction.

The power of IFS lies in its compassionate, empowering, and holistic approach to healing. By recognizing and honoring all parts of ourselves, we can transform our internal dynamics, cultivate self-leadership, and foster deep, lasting healing.

In the next chapter, we'll introduce the concept of somatic therapies and explain how the wisdom of the body can be combined with IFS for profound therapeutic results.

Chapter 2: Somatic Therapies: A Gateway to the Body

Somatic therapies are an integral part of the holistic therapeutic approach, centering on the critical interconnection between mind and body. As our body bears the marks of our experiences and emotions, engaging the body in the healing process is an essential step toward wholeness.

This chapter will introduce you to the world of somatic therapies, their foundations, benefits, techniques, and their place in the landscape of therapeutic practices. Let's step into this fascinating journey of somatic exploration.

The Mind-Body Connection

The mind-body connection, a foundational concept in somatic therapies, is a concept that acknowledges the intricate and inseparable relationship between our mental and physical states. This perspective understands the body not as a machine that merely executes commands from the brain but as a dynamic entity that communicates with, influences, and is influenced by our mind.

The Biopsychosocial Model

The mind-body connection is often discussed in the context of the biopsychosocial model of health. This model proposes that biological, psychological, and social factors all play a significant role in human functioning in the context of disease or illness.

For example, chronic stress (a psychological factor) can lead to elevated cortisol levels (a biological factor), which can in turn increase the risk of various health problems, such as heart disease, depression, and anxiety. On the other hand, regular exercise (a biological factor) can reduce stress levels and improve mood (psychological factors).

Psychoneuroimmunology and Psychophysiology

The fields of psychoneuroimmunology and psychophysiology provide further evidence of the mind-body connection. Psychoneuroimmunology studies the relationship between psychological processes and the nervous and immune systems of the human body. It's been shown, for instance, that stress and negative emotions can weaken the immune system, making us more susceptible to illnesses.

Psychophysiology studies the way in which the body physically responds to mental processes. For example, experiencing fear or anxiety can trigger the fight-or-flight response, leading to physical symptoms such as rapid heart rate, shallow breathing, and heightened alertness.

The Role of Emotions

Emotions play a pivotal role in the mind-body connection. Our bodies respond to the way we think, feel, and act. This is often called the "body-mind connection." When you are stressed, anxious, or upset, your body tries to tell you that something isn't right. For example, high blood pressure or a stomach ulcer might develop after a particularly stressful event, such as the death of a loved one.

The somatic markers hypothesis developed by neurologist Antonio Damasio suggests that emotions are primarily physical in nature and that our body and mind use emotional cues to help us make decisions. Our bodies are involved in emotional processing, storing memories of emotions and their associated physiological states.

Implications for Therapy

Recognizing the mind-body connection has significant implications for therapy. Somatic therapies understand that our bodies hold onto emotional traumas and stresses, manifesting as physical symptoms like tension, pain, or discomfort. By working directly with the body (for instance, through techniques like breathing exercises, movement therapy, and touch therapy), somatic therapies aim to address these physical manifestations of emotional distress, promoting holistic healing and integration.

let's delve into some specific examples that highlight the profound mind-body connection:

Example 1: Stress and Physical Health

Imagine a person, we'll call her Lisa, who has recently taken on a high-stress job. With the increased workload and responsibility, she's feeling constantly anxious and overwhelmed. Over time, these prolonged periods of stress start affecting her physically. She experiences frequent headaches, her sleep quality diminishes leading to chronic fatigue, and her immune system weakens, making her more susceptible to colds and other illnesses. Here, Lisa's mental state (high stress and anxiety) has a direct, tangible impact on her physical health.

Example 2: Exercise and Mental Health

Now, consider another person, we'll call him Mark, who starts incorporating regular exercise into his daily routine. After a few weeks, he notices that his mood has significantly improved. He feels more energetic during the day, his self-esteem has increased, and he's able to handle stress more effectively. The physical activity (exercise) has had a profound positive effect on his mental health.

Example 3: Trauma and Bodily Responses

Another poignant example can be seen in cases of trauma. For instance, a war veteran might develop post-traumatic stress disorder (PTSD), where certain sounds, sights, or smells trigger intense physical reactions like a pounding heart, rapid breathing, or profuse sweating. These triggers can even cause flashbacks to the traumatic event. In this case, mental trauma has caused a severe physiological response.

Example 4: Emotion-Induced Physical Sensations

Think about how you feel when you're nervous - maybe your palms get sweaty, your heart races, or you feel a knot in your stomach. Or when you're embarrassed, you might blush or feel hot. These are examples of your body responding to your emotions.

Example 5: Therapeutic Outcomes

Finally, in a therapeutic context, consider a patient using somatic therapy techniques to cope with anxiety. By learning and practicing deep, controlled breathing exercises when anxious feelings arise, the person could effectively reduce the physical symptoms associated with their anxiety, such as a racing heart and rapid breathing. This showcases how a physical technique (deep breathing) can alleviate a psychological issue (anxiety).

These examples highlight the depth of the mind-body connection, illustrating how our mental and physical states continuously influence and respond to each other. This connection is key to understanding the effectiveness of somatic therapies and their role in promoting holistic healing and well-being.

In conclusion, the mind-body connection is a powerful concept that recognizes the deep interplay between our mental and physical experiences. It forms the basis for a holistic approach to health and wellbeing, one that addresses both psychological and physical dimensions of distress. In the next section, we'll explore somatic therapies in more detail, looking at how they leverage the mind-body connection to foster healing and wellbeing.

What Are Somatic Therapies?

The term 'somatic' stems from the Greek word 'soma,' which translates to 'living body.' Somatic therapies refer to a group of therapeutic practices that use the body-mind connection to facilitate healing and wellness. These therapies are based on the principle that our bodies do not merely exist to carry our brains around, but rather, they are active participants in our emotional and psychological experiences.

Somatic therapy rests on the premise that the body and mind are not separate entities, but are fundamentally interconnected. Our physical bodies carry the imprint of our emotional, psychological, and social experiences. When we experience trauma or prolonged stress, these experiences can manifest as physical symptoms or "body memories" that linger even after our minds may have moved on.

For instance, a person who has experienced a traumatic event may develop chronic muscle tension, digestive issues, or other physical symptoms. Even after the traumatic event is over, these physical symptoms can persist, serving as a tangible reminder of past distress.

Techniques in Somatic Therapy

Somatic therapy encompasses a wide range of techniques aimed at fostering mind-body integration. Here, we'll dive deeper into some of these techniques and explore how they can facilitate healing.

Somatic Experiencing

Developed by Dr. Peter Levine, somatic experiencing is a body-oriented approach to healing trauma and stress-related disorders. This technique guides individuals to notice their bodily sensations, from tension and discomfort to ease and relaxation, and to gently move through these sensations. This process allows the body to release trapped trauma or stress, facilitating a return to balance and wellness.

Breathwork

Breathwork refers to various techniques that involve consciously controlling the breath. This could involve practices like deep belly breathing, box breathing, or guided breathing exercises. By helping to calm the nervous system, regulate emotions, and anchor individuals in their physical experience, breathwork can be a powerful tool in the somatic therapy toolkit.

Movement Therapy

Movement therapies encompass a range of practices that use movement as a pathway to mind-body integration. This could include:

- **Dance/movement therapy:** This approach uses dance and movement to support emotional, cognitive, and physical integration. It can involve free-form movement, guided dance exercises, or simply moving in ways that feel good to the individual.

- **Yoga:** Yoga combines physical postures, breathing exercises, meditation, and ethical principles to promote mind-body-spirit integration. Therapeutic forms of yoga can be particularly beneficial for trauma healing.

- **Tai chi or qigong:** These ancient Chinese practices involve slow, controlled movements, deep breathing, and meditation to cultivate balance and energy flow in the body.

Body Awareness Exercises

These exercises aim to cultivate a deeper awareness of the body and its sensations. This might involve mindfulness practices like body scans, where individuals are guided to slowly bring their attention to different parts of their bodies, noticing any sensations that arise without judgment. By increasing body awareness, these exercises can help individuals to recognize and release stored tension or trauma.

Touch Therapies

With the client's consent, some somatic therapists may use touch as part of the therapeutic process. This could involve:

- **Massage or bodywork:** These techniques can help release muscular tension, improve body awareness, and facilitate the release of stored trauma.

- **Craniosacral therapy:** This gentle, hands-on approach works with the bones of the skull and the sacrum to support the flow of cerebrospinal fluid and promote overall wellness.

- **Hakomi Method:** This body-centered psychotherapy method combines touch with mindfulness and nonviolence to explore unconscious patterns and facilitate change.

Let's explore some specific examples illustrating how these somatic therapy techniques might be used:

Example 1: Somatic Experiencing

John has a fear of heights which developed after a traumatic experience of falling from a tree in his childhood. His therapist guides him through a somatic experiencing process. The therapist asks John to visualize climbing the tree and notice the physical sensations that arise. As John acknowledges his shaky hands and rapid heartbeat, the therapist guides him to stay with these sensations, breathe into them, and gradually allow them to subside. This process helps John to gradually desensitize his body's response to the fear, eventually allowing him to feel safer in high places.

Example 2: Breathwork

Anna struggles with severe anxiety. During panic attacks, her breath becomes shallow, and she feels like she's choking. Her therapist teaches her a breathwork technique known as "box breathing" – breathe in for a count of four, hold for four, breathe out for four, and hold for four. The next time Anna begins to feel a panic attack coming on, she applies this technique. Her breath slows down, her heart rate drops, and she feels more grounded and less anxious.

Example 3: Movement Therapy

Peter, a war veteran with PTSD, finds traditional talk therapy challenging. He often feels disconnected from his emotions and struggles to articulate his experiences. His therapist suggests incorporating dance/movement therapy into their sessions. During these sessions, Peter is encouraged to express his feelings through movement. This form of therapy helps Peter connect with and express his emotions in a non-verbal way, providing an outlet for his trauma.

Example 4: Body Awareness Exercise

Sarah struggles with chronic tension headaches. Her therapist guides her through a body scan, asking her to notice any areas of tension or discomfort in her body. As Sarah brings her attention to her shoulders, she realizes they're hunched and tense. With this awareness, she's able to consciously relax her shoulders and decrease the tension contributing to her headaches.

Example 5: Touch Therapy

Thomas has trouble feeling connected to his body following a traumatic accident. His therapist, trained in Hakomi Method, uses mindful touch (with Thomas' consent) to help him reconnect with his body. As the therapist gently places a hand on Thomas' shoulder, Thomas begins to notice a sensation of warmth spreading through his body. This helps Thomas to start feeling more connected to his body and less detached from his physical experiences.

These examples showcase the diversity of somatic therapy techniques and illustrate how they can be applied to facilitate healing and wellness. Remember, somatic therapy is highly individual, and the specific techniques used should always be tailored to the unique needs and comfort level of the individual.

It's important to note that the specific techniques used in somatic therapy can vary widely depending on the therapist's training and the individual client's needs and comfort level. Always ensure that any therapy you engage in feels safe and appropriate for you. In the next section, we'll explore the benefits of somatic therapy and its potential for fostering deep, holistic healing.

Goals of Somatic Therapy

The ultimate goal of somatic therapy is to promote holistic healing and wellness by helping individuals reconnect with their bodies, process stored trauma, and integrate their bodily experiences with their emotions, thoughts, and behaviors. This can lead to improved self-awareness, better emotional regulation, reduced physical symptoms, and increased overall wellbeing.

In the context of Internal Family Systems therapy, somatic techniques can be a valuable tool for accessing and healing parts, particularly for individuals who might find it challenging to engage with their parts purely on a cognitive or emotional level. By incorporating the body into the therapy process, somatic therapies can help facilitate deeper, more holistic healing and integration.

The Benefits of Somatic Therapy

Somatic therapy can be particularly effective in treating trauma and stress-related conditions. By helping individuals release trapped trauma from their bodies, somatic therapy can alleviate physical symptoms and foster emotional healing. It can enhance self-awareness, improve emotional regulation, reduce anxiety and depression, and foster a greater sense of embodiment and wholeness.

In the context of Internal Family Systems therapy, somatic techniques can provide another pathway to access and heal parts, particularly for individuals who find it challenging to engage with their parts purely on a cognitive or emotional level.

In the following chapters, we'll explore how somatic therapy and IFS can be integrated to create a powerful, holistic approach to healing and personal growth. But first, let's delve deeper into the world of somatic techniques, understanding how each one can contribute to the journey toward wholeness.

Chapter 3: The Fusion

Now that we've established the fundamental concepts of Internal Family Systems (IFS) Therapy and Somatic Therapy, it's time to unveil the revolutionary approach that marries these two modalities: Somatic Internal Family Systems Therapy.

In this chapter, we'll explore how these two therapeutic approaches can be fused together to enhance their potential for healing and personal growth. We'll look at how the combination of IFS's focus on parts and Self, with the body-oriented techniques of Somatic Therapy, can lead to deeper insight, greater self-awareness, and holistic integration.

This approach is not merely about adding bodywork into an IFS session, but rather, it's about creating a synergistic fusion where each approach enhances the other, resulting in a powerful new modality for mind-body healing.

Somatic Internal Family Systems Therapy

Somatic Internal Family Systems Therapy is an innovative therapeutic approach that blends the principles and techniques of Internal Family Systems Therapy with the body-focused practices of Somatic Therapy. In doing so, it seeks to leverage the unique strengths of both modalities to facilitate deeper, more holistic healing.

Traditional Internal Family Systems Therapy posits that the mind is made up of distinct subpersonalities or "parts" and the Self. Each part carries its own perspectives, emotions, memories, and even physical sensations, and they may take on extreme roles in response to trauma or unmet needs. The goal of IFS is to help individuals access their Self, which embodies qualities of compassion, curiosity, and calmness, and from this place, heal and integrate their parts.

Somatic Therapy, on the other hand, is grounded in the understanding of the profound mind-body connection. It recognizes that our bodies are not mere vessels for our minds, but are intrinsically entwined with our mental and emotional experiences. Somatic therapy techniques help individuals cultivate body awareness, release stored tension or trauma, and integrate their physical experiences with their emotions, thoughts, and behaviors.

Somatic Internal Family Systems Therapy merges these two approaches, providing a way to work with parts not only at the mental and emotional level, but also at the physical level. In this way, it recognizes that parts may manifest not only as thoughts, emotions, and beliefs, but also as physical sensations, tensions, or discomforts.

In Somatic IFS Therapy, the therapist guides the individual to notice and explore their bodily sensations as a way to access and work with their parts. For example, a tightness in the chest might be explored as a part holding fear, while a heaviness in the shoulders might be a part carrying a burden. Through a combination of IFS techniques and somatic practices, these parts can be understood, comforted, and eventually integrated from a place of Self-leadership.

The result is a therapeutic approach that harnesses the wisdom of both the mind and the body, providing a powerful tool for healing and integration. By recognizing and honoring the physical manifestations of parts, Somatic IFS Therapy can help individuals connect more deeply with their parts, fostering a greater sense of wholeness and wellbeing.

The Benefits of Combining IFS and Somatic Therapies

The fusion of Internal Family Systems (IFS) and Somatic Therapies into Somatic Internal Family Systems Therapy leverages the strengths of both modalities and provides a multitude of benefits for individuals seeking healing and personal growth.

1. **Holistic Integration:** By working with both the mind and the body, Somatic IFS offers a more holistic approach to therapy. It recognizes that our experiences are stored not only in our minds but also in our bodies. By engaging both these aspects, Somatic IFS facilitates a more comprehensive and profound healing process.

2. **Access to Nonverbal Parts:** Some parts may find it difficult to express their experiences in words. They

might communicate more effectively through bodily sensations or movements. By incorporating somatic techniques, Somatic IFS provides an avenue for these nonverbal parts to express themselves and be understood.

3. **Enhanced Self-Awareness:** Somatic techniques can help individuals cultivate a greater awareness of their bodily sensations, which can provide additional insight into their parts and their internal system as a whole. This enhanced self-awareness can foster a deeper connection with the Self and promote greater self-understanding and self-compassion.

4. **Physiological Regulation:** Somatic therapies are known for their capacity to help regulate the nervous system, especially in cases of trauma. By incorporating these techniques, Somatic IFS can help individuals manage symptoms of stress, anxiety, and trauma, promoting greater physical and emotional well-being.

5. **Greater Accessibility:** For some individuals, conventional talk therapy can feel intimidating or inaccessible. The inclusion of body-based techniques in Somatic IFS can make the therapy process more engaging and approachable, potentially encouraging more individuals to seek help.

6. **Deepened Healing:** Somatic IFS acknowledges the physical manifestations of parts, which can sometimes be overlooked in conventional talk therapy. By recognizing and working with these physical manifestations, individuals can deepen their healing process, potentially leading to more lasting and impactful change.

7. **Enhanced Mind-Body Connection:** By highlighting the integral relationship between mind and body, Somatic IFS can help individuals enhance their mind-body connection, fostering greater overall wellness, self-awareness, and self-care habits.

The benefits of Somatic Internal Family Systems Therapy are numerous and far-reaching. By offering a synergistic blend of IFS and somatic therapies, this approach holds immense potential for profound, holistic healing and integration.

Techniques in Somatic IFS Therapy

In Somatic Internal Family Systems Therapy, the power of Internal Family Systems (IFS) and Somatic Therapy is harnessed to offer a transformative therapeutic approach. This approach uses various techniques from both modalities, bringing them together to form a robust toolbox for mind-body healing.

Here are some of the techniques that might be used in Somatic IFS Therapy:

Mindful Self-Exploration

A core practice in both IFS and Somatic Therapy, mindful self-exploration involves turning one's attention inward to explore one's internal experience. This might involve identifying parts and their roles, as well as noticing any associated physical sensations.

For example, if a client notices a feeling of sadness, the therapist might guide them to explore this feeling more deeply: "Where do you feel that sadness in your body? What does it feel like? Is there a part of you associated with that feeling?"

Somatic Awareness

Somatic awareness involves cultivating an awareness of the body and its sensations. This might involve noticing areas of tension or relaxation, changes in breath, or sensations associated with specific emotions or parts.

For example, the therapist might guide the client to notice how their body responds when they are in contact with different parts. They might ask, "As you connect with this protective part, what do you notice in your body? Are there any sensations, movements, or impulses that you become aware of?"

Parts Dialogue

In Somatic IFS Therapy, clients are guided to engage in dialogue with their parts, not only at a mental and emotional level but also at a physical level. This might involve asking parts to express their needs, fears, or desires, and paying attention to any associated physical responses.

For example, the therapist might guide the client to ask a part about its role: "Can you ask this part why it's holding so much tension in your shoulders? What is it trying to protect you from?"

Somatic Release

Somatic release involves using somatic techniques to help parts release stored tension or trauma. This might involve guided breathing exercises, movement, or mindful touch (with the client's consent).

For example, if a client has a part that is manifesting as a tightness in the chest, the therapist might guide them through a breathing exercise to help release that tension: "Can you bring your breath to this part in your chest? Imagine sending it warmth and relaxation with each exhale."

Compassionate Self-Leadership

In Somatic IFS Therapy, the goal is to help the client access their Self and lead their system from this place of compassion, curiosity, and calm. This often involves helping the client develop practices of self-compassion and self-care, both mentally and physically.

For example, the therapist might guide the client to send compassionate messages to their parts: "Can you send a message to this part that's holding fear in your stomach? Let it know that you see it, you appreciate its efforts to protect you, and that it's safe to relax now."

Through these techniques, Somatic IFS Therapy provides a comprehensive and effective approach to mind-body healing and integration. The exact techniques used may vary depending on the client's needs, preferences, and comfort level, but the goal remains the same: to facilitate a deep and holistic healing process.

Examples of Somatic IFS Therapy in Action

To help illustrate how Somatic Internal Family Systems Therapy can be applied, here are a few examples:

Example 1: Working with a Protective Part

Emily has a part that causes her to overwork, leading to burnout. During her therapy session, she notices a sensation of tightness in her shoulders and upper back whenever she thinks about work. Her therapist guides her to bring her attention to this sensation and ask it if it's a part. The tension confirms it's a part, and it's there to ensure Emily is successful and secure. Emily communicates with the part from her Self, assuring it she appreciates its protective nature, but she wants to find a healthier balance in life. The part relaxes, and so does the tension in Emily's shoulders.

Example 2: Releasing Traumatic Stress

Jake, a veteran, struggles with PTSD. His therapist guides him through a Somatic IFS session. Jake identifies a part that constantly feels on high alert, manifesting as a tight knot in his stomach. The therapist helps Jake mindfully approach this part, express appreciation for its vigilance, and gently ask if it would be willing to release some of the tension it's holding. Over time, with reassurance from Jake's Self, the part gradually begins to relax, and Jake's physical discomfort lessens.

Example 3: Healing Emotional Pain

Anna has recently ended a difficult relationship and frequently feels a heavy, aching sensation in her chest. Her therapist suggests this could be a part carrying heartache and invites Anna to get curious about it. As Anna dialogues with this part, she learns it's holding onto sadness and feelings of rejection. Anna acknowledges these feelings, thanks the part for allowing her to feel and process these emotions, and offers it reassurance. With this acknowledgment and comfort, the part begins to feel less intense, and the aching in Anna's chest starts to subside.

Example 4: Handling Anxiety

David is struggling with anxiety, often experiencing rapid heartbeats and a sense of unease. Through Somatic IFS, he identifies these sensations as parts carrying his fear and worry. He communicates with these parts from his Self, acknowledging their fear and asking them to ease the intense physical symptoms. This process helps reduce his anxiety levels, both emotionally and physically.

Example 5: Addressing Chronic Pain

Sarah has lived with chronic back pain for years, with no apparent physical cause. Her therapist helps her approach the pain as a part, and she discovers it carries feelings of being unsupported in life. By addressing these feelings, Sarah helps the part to release some of its tension, leading to a decrease in her chronic pain.

Example 6: Resolving Body Image Issues

Tom has a negative body image and often feels a sense of disgust when looking in the mirror. His therapist guides him to recognize this disgust as a part. Through dialogue and somatic awareness, Tom learns this part developed during childhood due to bullying. He reassures this part, helping it shift its perspective and easing his body image issues.

Example 7: Overcoming Insomnia

Samantha struggles with insomnia. During a Somatic IFS session, she realizes a part is keeping her awake, worrying about things that might go wrong. By addressing this part's concerns and reassuring it from her Self, Samantha manages to reduce its fears, leading to improved sleep.

Example 8: Healing from Grief

After the death of his wife, Mike experiences a heavy sensation in his heart. Recognizing this as a part holding his grief, Mike dialogues with it, acknowledging its pain and providing it with comfort. This process allows Mike to move through his grief more effectively.

Example 9: Conquering Phobias

Lucy has an irrational fear of driving, which she recognizes as a part stuck in the moment of a past car accident. By working with this part, Lucy manages to release the held fear and trauma from her body, eventually overcoming her phobia.

Example 10: Treating Depression

James has been diagnosed with depression and often feels a heavy weight pressing down on him. Through Somatic IFS, he identifies this weight as a part carrying his sadness and despair. By acknowledging and working with this part, James gradually lightens the weight of his depression.

Example 11: Processing Childhood Trauma

Ella carries childhood trauma, often feeling a choking sensation in her throat when she tries to speak about her past. Her therapist helps her identify this sensation as a part that's afraid of her speaking out. By reassuring this part from her Self, Ella eventually processes her trauma, and the choking sensation lessens.

These examples demonstrate how Somatic IFS Therapy can be a powerful tool for addressing both mental and physical aspects of our experiences. By engaging the body in the therapeutic process, Somatic IFS provides a holistic approach to healing and integration.

 These examples also show the wide range of issues that Somatic IFS Therapy can address, demonstrating the adaptability and comprehensive nature of this approach.

Overcoming Challenges in Somatic IFS Therapy

As with any therapeutic approach, Somatic Internal Family Systems (IFS) Therapy may present certain challenges. These can include difficulties in accessing parts or the Self, resistance from protective parts, intense emotional or physical reactions, and practical barriers such as time and cost. Below, we'll delve into these challenges and suggest ways to overcome them.

Difficulty Accessing Parts or the Self

One of the most common challenges in Somatic IFS Therapy is difficulty accessing parts or the Self. This can often occur if a person has experienced trauma or has a history of ignoring or suppressing their feelings.

Overcoming This Challenge

Patience and gentle exploration are key here. The therapist should guide the client to turn their attention inward, fostering a sense of curiosity and compassion. This process may take time, and it's important not to rush it. The use of somatic techniques such as mindful body scans or breathwork may aid in cultivating this inward connection.

Resistance from Protective Parts

Protective parts can sometimes resist the therapy process. They may fear that their vulnerabilities will be exposed, or they may be concerned about the potential for pain if exiled parts are accessed.

Overcoming This Challenge

Building trust is crucial. The therapist can guide the client to communicate with their protective parts, expressing appreciation for their role and providing reassurance. It may also be helpful to negotiate with these parts, asking them to step back temporarily to allow other parts to be accessed.

Intense Emotional or Physical Reactions

Sometimes, working with parts can lead to intense emotional or physical reactions. This might occur when a part is carrying a particularly painful memory or emotion, or when a part that has been exiled or ignored for a long time is finally given attention.

Overcoming This Challenge

The therapist can provide grounding techniques and self-soothing strategies to help the client manage these intense reactions. They can also remind the client that they can control the pace of the therapy and can take a break or step back if they need to.

Practical Barriers

Practical challenges such as time, cost, or geographical distance can also present hurdles to engaging in Somatic IFS Therapy.

Overcoming This Challenge

Flexible therapy options such as online sessions can help to address geographical barriers. For time and cost considerations, short-term focused therapy can be effective. Some therapists may also offer sliding scale fees or have a certain number of low-cost slots available.

Examples of Overcoming Challenges in Somatic IFS Therapy

Example 1: Difficulty Accessing Parts or the Self

Jane has always been a very analytical person, disconnected from her emotions. When her therapist introduces her to Somatic IFS Therapy, she struggles to access her parts or identify the Self. Her therapist encourages her to start with small steps, like noticing any bodily sensations when she experiences strong emotions.

Over time, Jane learns to recognize and access her parts, making progress in her therapy.

Example 2: Resistance from Protective Parts

Steve has a protective part that tries to maintain control at all times to ensure his safety. This part initially resists the therapy process, fearing it will lose control. Steve's therapist guides him to communicate with this part, acknowledging its role and asking for its cooperation. After several sessions, this protective part begins to trust the process and steps back, allowing Steve to access other parts.

Example 3: Intense Emotional or Physical Reactions

During a therapy session, Maria contacts a part that carries deep sadness from her childhood. As soon as she accesses this part, she feels an overwhelming wave of emotion and a sharp pain in her chest. Her therapist helps her use grounding techniques, such as focusing on her breath and the sensation of her feet on the floor, to manage this intense reaction.

Example 4: Practical Barriers

John is interested in Somatic IFS Therapy, but he lives in a remote area with no therapists nearby. He finds a therapist who offers online sessions, enabling him to participate in the therapy from the comfort of his home.

Example 5: Financial Constraints

Sarah is a student with a limited budget, but she wants to try Somatic IFS Therapy to address her anxiety. She finds a therapist who offers a sliding scale payment option, making the therapy more affordable for her.

Example 6: Difficulty in Discerning Parts

Oliver, a first-time client in therapy, finds it difficult to discern his parts or recognize the voice of the Self. The therapist encourages Oliver to gently focus on his physical sensations and emotions, understanding that this process takes time. Through consistent practice, Oliver gradually begins to identify different parts and hear the voice of the Self.

Example 7: Resistance from Strong Protective Parts

Laura encounters a strong protective part that resists engaging in dialogue during her therapy sessions. This part is fearful that exposing vulnerable or exiled parts will lead to pain and hurt. The therapist helps Laura to patiently reassure this protective part that its role is valued. Over time, this part becomes less resistant, allowing Laura to access other aspects of her internal system.

Example 8: Strong Physical Reactions

During a session, Adam comes into contact with a part that carries anger. As he starts to engage with this part, he experiences intense physical reactions such as a rapid heartbeat and hot flushes. Adam's therapist guides him through grounding techniques such as deep, mindful breathing and progressive muscle relaxation, which help him manage these reactions.

Example 9: Limited Access to Therapists

Lisa lives in a small town with limited access to therapists who practice Somatic IFS. To overcome this challenge, Lisa finds an experienced therapist who offers virtual sessions, enabling her to benefit from this therapeutic approach despite her geographical constraints.

Example 10: Time Constraints

Miguel has a busy schedule and struggles to find the time for regular therapy sessions. His therapist works with him to schedule shorter, but more frequent sessions. This allows Miguel to engage consistently in therapy without disrupting his routine.

These examples illustrate how therapists and clients can collaborate to navigate potential challenges in Somatic IFS Therapy, ensuring that clients can fully engage with and benefit from this therapeutic approach.

Despite these challenges, the benefits of Somatic IFS Therapy often outweigh the difficulties. By navigating these obstacles with patience, understanding, and flexibility, clients and therapists can maximize the potential of this holistic therapeutic approach.

Somatic IFS Therapy: A Path to Wholeness
The Concept of Wholeness

Wholeness, in the context of Somatic Internal Family Systems (IFS) Therapy, is the state of harmonious integration where all parts of the self are acknowledged, valued, and their needs met. It implies not the absence of multiple parts, but the recognition of these parts and their roles, leading to a healthy relationship among them and with the Self.

Wholeness is not about eliminating parts of ourselves that we may find difficult or uncomfortable. Instead, it is about nurturing a compassionate relationship with these parts, understanding their intentions, and helping them to transform and heal. This creates an internal balance, a sense of calm and acceptance, which often translates into improved physical and emotional health, enhanced resilience, and more fulfilling relationships.

Somatic IFS Therapy as a Path to Wholeness

Somatic IFS Therapy offers a unique pathway to wholeness, integrating the wisdom of the body with the transformative potential of IFS. This approach acknowledges the interconnectedness of mind and body, recognizing that our physical sensations and movements often reflect our inner parts.

Through the process of identifying and connecting with our parts, we can begin to understand their roles and intentions, acknowledge their feelings, and address their needs. By engaging the body in this process, we can gain deeper insights and often access parts that may be difficult to reach through traditional talk therapies alone.

Somatic techniques such as mindful body scanning, breathwork, or movement exercises can help to ground the therapeutic process, facilitating a deeper connection with the body and its wisdom. They can also provide a powerful tool for managing intense emotions or physical sensations associated with particular parts.

The Journey Toward Wholeness

The journey toward wholeness in Somatic IFS Therapy is a process, often involving several stages:

1. **Identifying Parts and the Self**: This involves developing awareness of our internal parts and beginning to distinguish them from the Self.

2. **Building Relationships with Parts**: This includes developing a compassionate, curious, and non-judgmental relationship with each part, recognizing its role and intentions.

3. **Unburdening and Healing Parts**: As parts begin to trust the Self, they may reveal burdens they carry - painful emotions, memories, or beliefs. The Self can then help these parts to release these burdens and heal.

4. **Integration**: This is the process of bringing all parts into a harmonious relationship with the Self and

with each other, fostering a sense of internal balance and wholeness.

By integrating the wisdom of the body with the transformative potential of IFS, Somatic IFS Therapy offers a powerful, holistic approach to healing and integration, promoting a sense of wholeness and well-being.

In the subsequent sections, we will delve deeper into each topic, providing a comprehensive understanding of Somatic Internal Family Systems Therapy and how it can pave the way to profound personal healing and growth.

Chapter 4: The Groundbreaking Approach

This chapter will outline the comprehensive step-by-step process of Somatic IFS, providing a roadmap for both therapists and individuals seeking a transformative journey towards wholeness. It covers everything from the initial steps of establishing safety and connection, exploring and identifying parts, to the final stages of unburdening and integrating the system. Throughout this chapter, we will also highlight the benefits of each step and provide practical examples to illustrate them.

Establishing Safety and Connection

Safety and connection serve as foundational elements of Somatic Internal Family Systems (IFS) Therapy. Without these two pillars, the therapy can't proceed effectively. This stage is about creating a secure environment that encourages openness and promotes mindful self-awareness. It often involves three key steps: building the therapeutic alliance, connecting with the Self, and establishing bodily awareness.

Building the Therapeutic Alliance

The therapeutic alliance, or the bond between therapist and client, is a key factor in successful therapy. The therapist works to create a non-judgmental, supportive space that facilitates the client's openness and willingness to explore their internal world.

Example: A therapist might spend the first few sessions getting to know the client, understanding their background, experiences, and goals for therapy. This might involve asking open-ended questions, expressing empathy, and providing reassurance about the confidentiality and boundaries of the therapy process.

Connecting with the Self

An integral part of Somatic IFS is fostering the client's connection with their Self, which is often described as the "seat of consciousness" characterized by qualities like compassion, curiosity, clarity, calm, confidence, courage, creativity, and connectedness (the 8 C's of Self). This connection provides a resourceful, steady base from which clients can explore and interact with their parts.

Example: A therapist might guide the client in a meditation to help them tap into their Self. This could involve asking the client to visualize a place where they feel peaceful and safe, prompting them to connect with feelings of calmness and compassion – qualities of the Self.

Establishing Bodily Awareness

In Somatic IFS, the body is seen as a crucial source of information about parts. Thus, establishing a connection with the body is an essential early step. This is often facilitated through somatic techniques, such as mindful body scanning or grounding exercises, which help clients tune into their bodily sensations and become more present.

Example: A therapist could guide the client through a body scan exercise, asking them to bring their attention to different parts of their body and notice any sensations, such as tension, tingling, warmth, or numbness. This not only helps the client connect with their body, but also can reveal initial clues about parts that might be holding tension or other sensations in the body.

Establishing safety and connection in Somatic IFS Therapy is a vital preliminary step that lays the groundwork for the exploration and transformation of the client's internal system. It fosters the necessary trust, mindfulness, and body awareness that underpin the entire therapeutic process.

Exploring and Identifying Parts

The exploration and identification of parts is a core process in Somatic Internal Family Systems (IFS) Therapy. This step involves recognizing and acknowledging the different parts that make up a client's internal system. Each part is understood to have its own perspective, feelings, memories, and goals, as well as unique ways of expressing itself through thoughts, feelings, and bodily sensations.

Recognizing the Presence of Parts

The first aspect of this process involves helping the client recognize the presence of different parts. This often starts with awareness of thoughts, feelings, or behaviors that seem to contradict each other or cause inner conflict.

Example: A client might express a desire to be more assertive at work, yet also feel an intense fear of confrontation. The therapist might guide the client to recognize that these conflicting feelings could be related to different parts: one that wants to assert boundaries and another that fears potential conflict.

Identifying Parts and Their Roles

Once the client begins to recognize the presence of different parts, the next step is to identify them and understand their roles. The therapist guides the client to explore the origins, beliefs, emotions, and intentions of each part, always approaching with curiosity and compassion.

Example: In exploring the part that fears confrontation, the client might discover that it is protecting them from potential rejection or conflict. This part might have developed in response to past experiences where asserting themselves led to negative outcomes. The therapist can help the client understand that this part is trying to protect them, even if its method of protection might be causing challenges in their current life.

Understanding Bodily Manifestations of Parts

Somatic IFS Therapy adds another layer to this process by integrating the body's wisdom. The therapist helps the client to tune into their body and notice any physical sensations that might be associated with a particular part.

Example: When focusing on the part that fears confrontation, the client might notice a tightness in their chest or a feeling of their stomach "dropping". These bodily sensations provide further information about the part and how it manifests within the client's experience.

Exploring and identifying parts in Somatic IFS Therapy is a delicate, collaborative process that requires the therapist's guidance and the client's openness to self-exploration. It is through this process that the client gains a nuanced understanding of their internal system, setting the stage for the transformative work of unburdening and integration.

Developing Relationships with Parts

After identifying the different parts, the next phase of Somatic Internal Family Systems (IFS) Therapy involves cultivating relationships with them. This process is critical for understanding the intentions of parts, helping them release their burdens, and integrating them into the overall system.

Initiating Dialogue with Parts

The relationship-building process often starts with initiating dialogue with each part. The therapist guides the client in communicating directly with their parts, expressing curiosity about their roles and intentions. This communication generally happens internally but may be expressed verbally in therapy.

Example: A client may engage with a part that often feels anxious. By asking open, non-judgmental questions like "What are you worried about?" or "What do you want me to understand?" the client can start to understand the part's fears and concerns.

Cultivating Compassion for Parts

One of the primary goals of IFS is to foster a compassionate relationship between the Self and each part. This involves acknowledging the part's experiences and validating its feelings, without trying to change or eliminate it.

Example: A client might feel frustrated with a part that constantly criticizes them. The therapist might guide the client to understand this part's protective intentions - perhaps it is trying to prevent disappointment or failure. Acknowledging the part's role and expressing appreciation can help cultivate compassion, even if its methods are problematic.

Encouraging Cooperation Among Parts

Once relationships have been established with individual parts, the therapist guides the client to foster cooperation among them. This involves recognizing the shared goal of all parts, which is to protect and support the client, even if their methods differ.

Example: A client may have one part that urges them to work harder (to ensure success) and another part that encourages relaxation (to protect against burnout). The therapist can help the client understand that both parts have their well-being in mind. By fostering dialogue between these parts, the client can work towards a balance that satisfies both needs.

Incorporating Somatic Awareness

As in all steps of Somatic IFS, this phase also integrates somatic awareness. The client is encouraged to notice how their body reacts as they interact with each part, providing another layer of insight into their internal system.

Example: As a client engages with a part that holds sadness, they might notice a heaviness in their chest. This somatic experience can inform the therapeutic process, offering a tangible, physical aspect to the part's emotional state.

Developing relationships with parts is an integral step in Somatic IFS Therapy. It sets the stage for the unburdening and integration process, allowing for a comprehensive, nuanced understanding of the client's internal system.

Unburdening Parts
Unburdening is a transformative phase in Somatic Internal Family Systems (IFS) Therapy. After developing relationships with different parts, the client is guided to help these parts release their burdens. Burdens are the extreme beliefs, emotions, or sensations that a part may carry, often rooted in traumatic or challenging experiences from the past.

Acknowledging the Burdens

The first step in the unburdening process is acknowledging the burdens that each part carries. This involves exploring the roots of these burdens and recognizing the pain, fear, or other negative emotions associated with them.

Example: A client may discover that a part carrying intense anxiety stems from childhood experiences of instability and unpredictability. The therapist guides the client to validate this part's fear and acknowledge the burden it has been carrying for years.

Expressing Permission for Unburdening

Before the unburdening can occur, it is essential to ensure all parts of the system are okay with the process. Any parts that are afraid or uncertain about the unburdening process can block it from happening.

Example: A client who is ready to unburden a part holding anger might find that another part is afraid of the potential loss of control. The therapist can facilitate a conversation between these parts, reassuring the protective part and addressing its concerns.

Guiding the Unburdening Process

The actual unburdening process is a guided release of the part's extreme beliefs, emotions, or sensations. This may involve visualization exercises, emotional expression, or somatic techniques.

Example: For a part holding guilt, the therapist might guide the client in a visualization where they return the guilt to where it originated or release it into a safe container. This visual exercise, coupled with mindful attention to bodily sensations, helps to facilitate the release of the burden.

Encouraging Self-Led Healing

The final step in the unburdening process involves the Self leading the healing. This can take the form of offering the part reassurances, compassion, and understanding. It reinforces the leadership of the Self in the internal system and promotes a sense of inner harmony.

Example: After a part has released a burden of shame, the client, from the Self, might offer this part reassurances like "You did the best you could at the time" or "You are not alone".

Unburdening in Somatic IFS Therapy is a powerful, liberating process that enables parts to let go of the burdens they've carried for so long. It paves the way for the integration of the parts and the overall healing of the client's internal system.

Integration and Restoration of the System

The final phase in Somatic Internal Family Systems (IFS) Therapy is the integration and restoration of the system. After identifying parts, building relationships with them, and helping them unburden, the client is guided to integrate these parts into their overall internal system. This process aims to foster inner harmony and wholeness.

Reassigning Roles

Once parts have been unburdened, they are often free to take on new roles within the system. Instead of being confined by their burdens, they can contribute in healthier, more beneficial ways.

Example: A part that was once critical and judgmental due to fear of failure might transform into a motivating force after it's unburdened, encouraging the client in a supportive way to reach their goals.

Fostering Internal Connection and Cooperation

Integration also involves promoting ongoing connection and cooperation among the parts and the Self. The goal is to create an internal system where all parts are valued and heard, and the Self leads with qualities of calmness, curiosity, compassion, clarity, confidence, courage, creativity, and connectedness.

Example: A client might continue to hold internal meetings, checking in with their parts regularly, acknowledging their contributions, and fostering dialogue among them. Over time, this can lead to a more harmonious and balanced internal system.

Somatic Integration

In Somatic IFS, the integration phase also incorporates the body. Clients are guided to notice changes in their bodily sensations as they integrate their parts, offering another layer of insight and healing.

Example: After unburdening and integrating a part that used to cause a persistent tightness in their chest, a client might notice a feeling of lightness or spaciousness in that area. This bodily change reflects the internal transformation that has taken place.

Restoration of the System

The ultimate goal of Somatic IFS Therapy is the restoration of the client's internal system. This means the Self leads, parts are free of their burdens and work in harmony, and the body and mind are aligned.

Example: After the process of Somatic IFS, a client might notice a significant shift in their overall wellbeing. They may experience less internal conflict, more emotional balance, better stress management, and a greater sense of peace and wholeness.

Integration and restoration in Somatic IFS Therapy mark the culmination of a transformative journey. This phase illustrates the groundbreaking potential of this therapeutic approach, highlighting its capacity to foster wholeness, harmony, and a deep sense of internal peace.

Throughout this chapter, we will delve into each of these steps in more detail, providing practical guidance and examples to help you understand and navigate the transformative journey that is Somatic IFS Therapy.

Chapter 5: Techniques of Somatic IFS

Somatic Internal Family Systems (IFS) Therapy integrates the principles of IFS with somatic (body-based) practices to facilitate a holistic healing process. This unique fusion allows for a more comprehensive approach to therapy that takes into account the interconnectedness of mind, body, and spirit. This chapter will delve into various techniques of Somatic IFS, offering practical guidance for both therapists and individuals interested in this approach.

Somatic Awareness and Exploration

Somatic awareness and exploration refer to the conscious attention and inquiry into the body's sensations, feelings, and movements. It's the process of connecting to the body and becoming aware of its signals and messages, which often mirror our internal emotional states.

The Role of Somatic Awareness in Somatic IFS

Somatic awareness serves as the foundation for Somatic Internal Family Systems (IFS) Therapy. As we bring conscious attention to our bodies, we begin to notice the subtle, and sometimes not-so-subtle, ways in which our internal parts express themselves physically.

In traditional IFS, parts are often identified through thoughts, emotions, images, or memories. In Somatic IFS, however, the identification process also includes noticing how each part manifests in the body. For instance, a protective part might cause tension in the shoulders, while an exiled part might be associated with a heaviness in the chest.

Practicing Somatic Awareness

Practicing somatic awareness involves deliberately tuning into your body. It can be as simple as noticing your breath—its rhythm, depth, and how it fills and leaves your body. Or it can involve a full-body scan, where you mentally traverse your body from head to toe, noting any sensations, discomfort, tension, or ease.

Examples of Somatic Awareness and Exploration

Example 1: A client notices a knot in their stomach whenever they think about a stressful situation at work. By paying attention to this sensation, they identify a part that feels overwhelmed by the stress.

Example 2: During a therapy session, a client experiences a sudden headache. Instead of dismissing it, the client and therapist explore this sensation. The client realizes it's a protective part stepping in, trying to distract them from feeling vulnerable.

Example 3: As part of their daily routine, a client spends a few minutes each morning checking in with their body. They notice a consistent tension in their jaw and decide to bring it up in their next therapy session. They discover it's connected to a part that's always on guard, ready to defend against criticism.

Somatic awareness and exploration provide an essential pathway into the subconscious mind. They help us discover our internal parts that might have been overlooked or ignored in more cognitive-based approaches. By incorporating the body into the therapy process, Somatic IFS offers a truly holistic approach to healing and integration.

Tracking Bodily Responses

In Somatic Internal Family Systems (IFS) Therapy, tracking bodily responses is an essential technique. It involves observing and recording changes in the body's sensations, feelings, or movements as a client engages with different parts or explores different experiences or memories. This technique helps therapists and clients better understand how parts manifest somatically and how they respond to various therapeutic interventions.

The Importance of Tracking Bodily Responses

The body's responses often provide valuable information about our internal emotional state and the dynamics of our parts. For instance, a change in bodily sensation can indicate the activation of a part, a shift in the relationship between parts, or the release of a burden.

By tracking these bodily responses, therapists and clients can gain deeper insights into the therapy process, facilitate somatic unburdening, and support the integration and healing of the system.

How to Track Bodily Responses

Tracking bodily responses involves a heightened awareness and focus on the body throughout the therapy session. Therapists might guide clients to notice any changes in sensations, feelings, or movements as they engage with different parts or recall different experiences. They might ask questions like "What are you noticing in your body right now?" or "How does your body respond when you connect with this part?"

Examples of Tracking Bodily Responses

Example 1: A client reports a tightening in their chest as they start to connect with a part holding sadness. This bodily response suggests that the part is active and possibly ready to communicate or unburden.

Example 2: During a therapy session, a client notices a sense of relief and relaxation in their body after they reassure a worried part. This change in bodily sensation indicates a positive shift in the client's internal system.

Example 3: A client experiences a spontaneous deep breath and softening in their shoulders when they visualize a protective part stepping back. This response suggests that the part has agreed to give space for the Self to lead.

Tracking bodily responses provides another layer of insight into the therapy process. It underscores the interconnectedness of mind and body and emphasizes the role of the body in healing and integration. In Somatic IFS

Therapy, it's not just about listening to our thoughts or emotions, but also tuning into our bodies' wisdom and guidance.

Grounding Techniques

Grounding techniques are strategies used in Somatic IFS therapy to help clients stay focused on the present moment and maintain a connection with their physical selves. These techniques can be particularly useful when clients are dealing with intense emotions or memories, as they can provide a sense of stability and safety.

The Role of Grounding Techniques in Somatic IFS

In Somatic Internal Family Systems (IFS) Therapy, grounding techniques serve as important tools to manage overwhelming or distressing feelings. These feelings can be triggered when clients connect with certain parts, especially exiles carrying burdens from traumatic or painful experiences. Grounding techniques can help clients avoid getting swept away by these feelings, fostering a safer therapeutic environment.

Various Grounding Techniques

Grounding techniques can be both physical and mental exercises, all aimed at helping the individual stay present and connected to their bodies. Here are a few examples:

- **Physical Grounding Techniques:** These may involve focusing on the breath, feeling the feet on the floor, or touching a tangible object.

- **Mental Grounding Techniques:** These can involve mindfulness exercises, such as observing the surroundings in detail or counting backward.

Examples of Grounding Techniques

Example 1: During a session, a client starts to feel anxious when connecting with a part that holds memories of a traumatic event. The therapist guides the client to focus on their breath, taking deep, slow inhalations and exhalations. This simple grounding technique helps the client calm their nervous system and return to the present moment.

Example 2: A client begins to feel dissociated when a protective part gets activated. The therapist instructs the client to feel their feet on the floor, noticing the firmness of the ground beneath them. This grounding technique helps the client regain their sense of connection with their body and the present moment.

Example 3: A client is struggling with intrusive thoughts linked to a burdened exile part. The therapist suggests a mental grounding technique: the client is asked to count backward from 100 by 7s, shifting their attention away from the intrusive thoughts and toward the counting task.

Grounding techniques, such as these, play a crucial role in maintaining safety and stability in Somatic IFS therapy. They help clients navigate challenging emotions and memories while keeping a firm connection with the present moment and their physical selves.

Somatic Dialogue

Somatic dialogue is a technique used in Somatic Internal Family Systems (IFS) therapy that incorporates the body's wisdom into the therapeutic process. This technique involves not just speaking to parts mentally or verbally, but also communicating with them through the body's sensations, movements, and impulses.

The Role of Somatic Dialogue in Somatic IFS

In Somatic IFS, the body is considered a gateway to understanding and healing our parts. Our parts not only influence our thoughts and feelings but also manifest in our bodies in various ways. By engaging in a somatic dialogue, we can gain additional insights into our parts, facilitate their healing, and support their integration.

Somatic dialogue can involve asking a part to intensify its physical manifestation to communicate its message, or inviting a part to release a burden through a physical gesture or movement. It can also involve sensing the body's intuitive responses to different parts or to various therapeutic interventions.

Examples of Somatic Dialogue

Example 1: A client notices a tightening sensation in their chest as they start to connect with a part. The therapist guides the client to engage in a somatic dialogue with this part, asking it to express its message through the chest tightening. The client finds that the tightening sensation intensifies when they recall a certain memory, suggesting that the part is connected to that experience.

Example 2: During a therapy session, a client identifies a protective part that manifests as tension in the shoulders. The therapist invites the client to dialogue with this part somatically, asking the part if it would be willing to relax the shoulders as a sign of stepping back. When the client does this, they notice a sense of relief and more openness to exploring their exiled parts.

Example 3: A client is working with a part that carries a burden of guilt. The therapist suggests that the client could invite the part to release this burden through a physical gesture, like shaking hands or taking a deep breath. As the client follows through with this somatic dialogue, they report feeling a sense of lightness and release.

Somatic dialogue offers a unique way to engage with parts, allowing them to express themselves not just through words or images but also through bodily sensations and movements. This body-based communication can provide deeper insights into the parts and their burdens, facilitating a more holistic healing and integration process.

Somatic Unburdening

Somatic unburdening is a critical component of Somatic Internal Family Systems (IFS) Therapy that involves releasing burdens that parts carry at a somatic level. In traditional IFS, unburdening typically refers to the process of releasing burdens in the form of painful beliefs, emotions, or memories. In Somatic IFS, unburdening extends to the physical dimension, recognizing that burdens can also manifest as tensions, pains, or discomforts in the body.

The Role of Somatic Unburdening in Somatic IFS

Somatic unburdening is essential for achieving true and lasting healing and integration in Somatic IFS. It acknowledges that our bodies hold onto traumas and stresses just as our minds do, and that releasing these somatic burdens is just as crucial as releasing emotional or mental burdens.

Somatic unburdening can involve physical movements or gestures, changes in body posture, or shifts in bodily sensations. These can symbolize the release of a burden and facilitate the transformation of a part.

Examples of Somatic Unburdening

Example 1: A client connects with a part that carries a burden of shame, which manifests as a heavy feeling in the chest. The therapist guides the client through a somatic unburdening process, inviting the part to release the shame through a physical gesture, like opening the chest wide. As the client does this, they report a lifting of the heaviness in their chest.

Example 2: During a therapy session, a client identifies a protective part that holds tension in the shoulders. The therapist supports the client in somatically unburdening this part, asking if it would be willing to let go of the tension. When the client allows their shoulders to relax and drop, they experience a sense of relief and calmness.

Example 3: A client is working with an exile part that holds a burden of fear, causing a knot in the stomach. The therapist suggests a somatic unburdening technique involving deep, slow belly breathing, which can help relax the stomach muscles and release the tension. As the client follows through with this technique, they notice the knot in their stomach starting to loosen.

Somatic unburdening provides a way for parts to release their burdens at a bodily level, offering a more holistic and comprehensive approach to healing. By including the body in the unburdening process, Somatic IFS recognizes the interconnectedness of mind and body and supports the integration of the whole self.

Integrating Somatic Changes

The integration of somatic changes is a final and pivotal step in the Somatic Internal Family Systems (IFS) therapeutic process. This process acknowledges that the body, just like the mind, carries memories and impacts of past traumas and stresses. The changes that occur in the body as a result of somatic unburdening and other therapeutic interventions need to be integrated into the client's overall sense of self to ensure comprehensive healing and wholeness.

The Role of Integrating Somatic Changes in Somatic IFS

In Somatic IFS, integration involves recognizing and validating the somatic changes that have occurred, incorporating these changes into the client's self-perception and self-experience, and allowing these changes to influence how the client interacts with themselves and the world.

The integration of somatic changes also helps to consolidate the healing and transformation achieved in therapy, making it more stable and enduring. It reinforces the new, healthier patterns of being and relating that the client has developed and supports their continued growth and development.

Examples of Integrating Somatic Changes

Example 1: A client has worked through a burden of fear held by an exiled part, which manifested as a chronic tightness in the chest. Through somatic unburdening, the client has been able to release this tightness. As part of the integration process, the client learns to recognize and appreciate the new sense of openness and lightness in their chest, reflecting a release of fear and a greater capacity for courage and vulnerability.

Example 2: A client has been dealing with a protective part that caused tension in the shoulders. After working through a process of somatic unburdening, the client's shoulders are now more relaxed. The client is guided to integrate this somatic change by consciously noting the lack of tension and interpreting it as a symbol of the protective part's trust and relaxation. They are also encouraged to maintain this relaxed posture in their day-to-day life, reinforcing the transformation that has occurred.

Example 3: A client has explored a part that manifested as stomach discomfort associated with anxiety. Through somatic dialogue and unburdening, the client has been able to alleviate this discomfort. The integration process involves the client acknowledging this change and recognizing it as a sign of reduced anxiety and increased calmness. They are also encouraged to adopt practices such as mindful eating and gentle abdominal exercises that can support this positive somatic change.

Integrating somatic changes is crucial in ensuring the full and lasting benefits of Somatic IFS therapy. It helps clients embody the healing and transformation they have achieved and supports them in living more integrated, whole, and fulfilling lives.

Chapter 6: Case Studies and Applications

We then delve into real-world applications of Somatic IFS. Here, we present various case studies demonstrating the efficacy of this approach in treating a range of mental health conditions. This chapter also includes reflective questions to encourage professionals and individuals to reflect on how Somatic IFS might work in their context.

Case Study 1: Treating Complex PTSD with Somatic IFS

Case Background: Grace is a 35-year-old woman who has been diagnosed with complex post-traumatic stress disorder (C-PTSD) stemming from repeated childhood abuse. She reports experiencing flashbacks, dissociation, chronic anxiety, and a persistent sense of shame and unworthiness.

Therapeutic Approach: Somatic IFS was employed as a means to facilitate Grace's healing. Her therapy began with building a relationship of safety and trust. The therapist invited Grace to ground herself using various somatic techniques such as deep belly breathing and sensing her feet on the ground.

Gradually, Grace was guided to identify her parts. She identified a protective part that kept her constantly vigilant and anxious, a manager part that strived for perfection to avoid criticism, and an exiled part that carried the burden of the childhood abuse.

Through somatic dialogue, Grace started to communicate with these parts, acknowledging their physical manifestations. She identified tension in her shoulders as a sign of her protective part's vigilance and a heaviness in her heart as a manifestation of her exiled part's pain.

Grace then worked on unburdening these parts somatically. For instance, she was invited to imagine the tension in her shoulders melting away, symbolizing her protective part's readiness to relax its constant vigilance. Over several sessions, Grace reported a decrease in shoulder tension and anxiety.

Outcome: Grace's therapeutic journey with Somatic IFS has resulted in significant improvements in her C-PTSD symptoms. She reports fewer flashbacks, reduced anxiety, and a growing sense of self-compassion and worthiness. The integration of somatic changes – like the reduced shoulder tension – has been a powerful reminder of her healing journey.

Reflective Questions:

- How did the somatic techniques support Grace's healing process?

- What were the challenges faced during this therapeutic journey and how were they addressed?

- How might Somatic IFS be adapted or used differently with other clients with C-PTSD?

Case Study 2: Addressing Generalized Anxiety Disorder with Somatic IFS

Case Background: John, a 42-year-old engineer, presented with chronic and pervasive anxiety that was impacting his work, relationships, and overall quality of life. He was diagnosed with Generalized Anxiety Disorder (GAD).

Therapeutic Approach: The Somatic IFS approach began with establishing safety and grounding. John learned techniques such as mindful body scanning to enhance his somatic awareness.

John identified several parts, including a worrying part that constantly anticipated negative outcomes and a self-critical part that maintained high standards. These parts often triggered physical symptoms like stomach knots and headaches.

Through somatic dialogue, John was able to communicate with these parts. He was guided to somatically unburden the worrying part by visualizing the stomach knots untangling. Similarly, for the self-critical part, John practiced releasing the tension associated with his headaches.

Outcome: After several months of therapy, John reported a significant reduction in his anxiety levels. He noticed that his stomach was often relaxed and his headaches less

frequent, signaling a somatic integration of his parts'
unburdening.

Reflective Questions:

- How did Somatic IFS contribute to John's
  management of GAD?

- What somatic techniques seemed most beneficial
  for John, and why?

- How might this approach differ for other clients
  with GAD?

Case Study 3: Overcoming Depression with Somatic IFS

Case Background: Emily, a 28-year-old teacher, had been
struggling with severe depression. She often felt lethargic,
disconnected, and had difficulty concentrating.

Therapeutic Approach: Emily began Somatic IFS therapy by
establishing a safe therapeutic environment. She learned
grounding techniques like deep, grounding breaths and
mindfulness.

Emily identified a heavy, oppressive part that carried
feelings of worthlessness and despair, which often
manifested as a weight on her chest. She also discovered
an overworked part that was constantly striving to prove
her worth.

Through somatic unburdening, Emily was guided to
envision the weight on her chest gradually lifting. For the

overworked part, Emily learned to sense the stress leaving her body through progressive muscle relaxation.

Outcome: Emily reported a significant improvement in her depressive symptoms. The physical sensation of heaviness was less frequent, and she felt more energy and motivation. These somatic changes were integrated into Emily's sense of self, contributing to her continued recovery.

Reflective Questions:

- How did the Somatic IFS approach address Emily's depressive symptoms?

- What were the significant somatic changes Emily experienced?

- How might the approach be adjusted for other clients with depression?

Case Study 4: Managing Obsessive-Compulsive Disorder with Somatic IFS

Case Background: Thomas, a 39-year-old writer, was diagnosed with Obsessive-Compulsive Disorder (OCD). He struggled with compulsive behaviors and intrusive thoughts that disrupted his life and career.

Therapeutic Approach: The therapy process commenced with the establishment of a safe therapeutic space. Thomas was taught grounding techniques, such as focusing on his breathing and becoming aware of the contact points between his body and the chair or the ground.

Thomas discovered a controlling part that was at the core of his compulsive behaviors and a fearful part that was the source of his anxiety and intrusive thoughts. These parts often manifested as tightness in his chest and trembling hands.

Using somatic dialogue, Thomas learned to communicate with these parts and understand their roles. He was guided to somatically unburden these parts by visualizing the tightness in his chest softening and his hands becoming steady and calm.

Outcome: After several months of therapy, Thomas reported that his compulsive behaviors and intrusive thoughts had decreased considerably. He also noticed that the tightness in his chest had diminished and his hands trembled less often, reflecting the somatic integration of the unburdened parts.

Reflective Questions:

- How did Somatic IFS address Thomas' OCD symptoms?

- What were the significant somatic changes that Thomas experienced?

- How could this therapeutic approach be adapted for other clients with OCD?

Case Study 5: Healing Trauma with Somatic IFS

Case Background: Sarah, a 30-year-old war veteran, was struggling with symptoms of Post-Traumatic Stress Disorder (PTSD). She had recurring nightmares, was hypervigilant, and often experienced flashbacks of traumatic events.

Therapeutic Approach: In her therapy sessions, Sarah learned several grounding techniques to help manage her symptoms and promote safety.

She identified an exiled part that carried the trauma of the war and a protective part that kept her in a state of hyper-vigilance. These parts manifested as a choking sensation in her throat and tension in her back.

Through somatic dialogue, Sarah learned to communicate with these parts, understanding their fears and needs. Somatic unburdening was done by guiding Sarah to visualize the choking sensation easing and the tension in her back releasing.

Outcome: Sarah reported a significant decrease in PTSD symptoms, including fewer nightmares and flashbacks. Her somatic symptoms also improved, with a reduction in the choking sensation and back tension, marking the integration of the unburdened parts.

Reflective Questions:

- How did Somatic IFS help Sarah manage her PTSD symptoms?

- What somatic changes did Sarah experience?

- How might this therapeutic approach be adapted for other trauma survivors?

Case Study 6: Coping with Stress and Burnout with Somatic IFS

Case Background: Alex, a 36-year-old startup founder, was dealing with chronic stress and burnout. He was constantly fatigued, had difficulty sleeping, and found it hard to enjoy activities he once loved.

Therapeutic Approach: Alex's therapy started with grounding exercises like deep breathing and body scanning to foster somatic awareness.

He identified a part that was driving him to work excessively and a depleted part that carried his exhaustion and burnout. These parts manifested as tightness in his jaw and an overwhelming sense of heaviness in his body.

Alex engaged in somatic dialogue with these parts, understanding their purpose and acknowledging their physical manifestations. Somatic unburdening techniques were employed, such as releasing the tightness in his jaw and inviting a sense of lightness into his body.

Outcome: Following therapy, Alex reported a significant decrease in stress levels and an improvement in his sleep and overall mood. He noted that the physical tightness in his jaw had diminished, and his body felt lighter and more energized, reflecting the integration of unburdened parts.

Reflective Questions:

- How did Somatic IFS help Alex manage his symptoms of burnout?

- What were the significant somatic changes that Alex experienced?

- How could this therapeutic approach be adapted for other clients struggling with burnout?

Case Study 7: Healing Relationship Trauma with Somatic IFS

Case Background: Maria, a 32-year-old graphic designer, had a history of troubled relationships. She experienced severe trust issues and found it hard to form meaningful connections due to past betrayals.

Therapeutic Approach: Maria began therapy by learning grounding techniques, which helped her manage her anxiety in the sessions.

Maria identified a part that was afraid of betrayal and another part that pushed people away to protect her from getting hurt. These parts manifested as a tight knot in her stomach and a closed-off sensation in her chest.

Through somatic dialogue and unburdening, Maria was guided to release the tight knot in her stomach and open up the closed-off feeling in her chest.

Outcome: After several therapy sessions, Maria noticed an improvement in her relationships. She felt more open to trust and intimacy. The physical sensations associated with her parts also eased, indicating the integration of unburdened parts.

Reflective Questions:

- How did Somatic IFS address Maria's relationship issues?

- What somatic changes did Maria experience?

- How might this therapeutic approach be adapted for other clients with relationship trauma?

Each of these case studies demonstrates the versatility and effectiveness of Somatic IFS in addressing a variety of mental health issues. In the following chapters, we will delve deeper into the potential applications and future of Somatic IFS.

Chapter 7: Toward Integration and Wholeness

Understanding Integration in Somatic IFS

Integration in the context of Somatic Internal Family Systems (IFS) Therapy is the holistic amalgamation of the mind, body, and spirit, achieved through the successful navigation of one's internal system and the harmonious co-existence of all parts led by the Self.

Psychological Integration

Psychological integration in IFS refers to the process by which an individual recognizes, understands, and accepts the multiple parts within themselves. It involves creating a space where all parts feel heard, valued, and welcome, ultimately enabling each part to relax into its non-extreme role.

This means no part is ignored, suppressed, or ostracized. Even the parts perceived as 'negative' or 'destructive' are acknowledged and understood for their protective roles. As parts start to trust the leadership of the Self, they let go of their extreme beliefs, feelings, and behaviors— a process known as unburdening.

A real-world example could be someone struggling with an addiction. They might recognize a 'part' that compulsively seeks the addictive substance (a firefighter), another 'part' that criticizes them for this behavior (a manager), and possibly a 'part' that carries pain leading to the addictive behavior (an exile). Through IFS therapy, they would learn to understand and empathize with these parts, gradually unburdening them and enabling healthier coping mechanisms.

Somatic Integration

Somatic integration is a distinctive aspect of Somatic IFS. It refers to the awareness and acceptance of the physical sensations, impulses, and responses associated with different parts.

The body holds memories and emotions, often manifesting them as physical symptoms. Somatic integration involves acknowledging these physical manifestations and working with them therapeutically. As the parts unburden, their associated physical symptoms may transform or even dissolve, further fostering the process of overall integration.

Consider someone carrying trauma from a past accident, which manifests as chronic pain in their leg. As they work with their parts related to this trauma, their leg pain might ease, reflecting the somatic integration process.

Spiritual Integration

Spiritual integration refers to the alignment of the Self with one's personal values, purpose, and belief systems. In IFS, the Self is seen as the spiritual core of an individual— a seat of consciousness characterized by qualities like calmness, curiosity, compassion, and clarity.

As an individual progresses through their Somatic IFS journey, they cultivate a stronger connection with their Self. This strengthened connection facilitates a sense of alignment with their deeper purpose and values, fostering a state of wholeness that transcends the psychological and physical realms.

Reflective Questions:

1. How do you understand the concept of integration in Somatic IFS?

2. What steps can you take towards psychological, somatic, and spiritual integration?

3. How can fostering integration enhance your journey towards wholeness and wellbeing?

The Journey Toward Wholeness

Embarking on a journey toward wholeness requires courage, patience, and persistence. It's a process that involves facing the often uncomfortable truths about ourselves and our past, acknowledging and accepting all aspects of our being—both the comfortable and the uncomfortable.

Recognizing the Parts

The first step on this journey involves recognizing the existence of different parts within us. This recognition is more than a mere intellectual understanding; it's an experiential understanding where we start to notice our internal dialogues, emotional swings, and body sensations as different parts expressing themselves.

For example, recognizing parts might involve becoming aware of a critical voice inside your head and realizing that it's just a part of you—an 'inner critic'—rather than your whole identity. You may also start to notice physical sensations associated with this part, like a feeling of constriction in your chest.

Acknowledging and Accepting Parts

Once we've recognized our parts, the next step is to acknowledge and accept them. This means allowing them to exist without trying to suppress, ignore, or change them.

Consider the example of the 'inner critic'. After recognizing it, you might find yourself trying to ignore or silence it. But, in IFS, we take a different approach. We listen to the 'inner critic', acknowledging its presence and accepting its role in our system.

Unburdening Parts

The ultimate goal of Somatic IFS is to unburden parts that carry extreme beliefs, emotions, or memories. Unburdening is a process that involves creating a safe space for parts to let go of their burdens.

In the context of Somatic IFS, unburdening may also involve a somatic or physical release. For example, the constriction in your chest associated with your 'inner critic' might start to ease as you work through the process of unburdening.

Building Relationships with Parts

Building relationships with our parts is crucial for fostering integration and wholeness. This process involves developing empathy for our parts, understanding their intentions, and creating space for them in our internal family.

This is an ongoing process that requires patience and compassion. It may involve regular 'check-ins' with our parts, intentional dialogues, and mindful attention to the physical sensations associated with different parts.

Embracing the Self

Ultimately, the journey toward wholeness is a journey toward the Self. As we unburden parts and build internal relationships, the Self—our core essence—begins to emerge.

When we are in Self, we experience a sense of calm, clarity, compassion, confidence, creativity, curiosity, and connectedness—the eight Cs of Self-leadership in IFS. This is the state of being that reflects true wholeness.

Reflective Questions:

- How have you experienced the journey toward wholeness in your life?

- How can you support your parts in their process of unburdening?

- What does embracing the Self mean to you?

Somatic IFS as a Path to Wholeness

Somatic Internal Family Systems (IFS) Therapy is a therapeutic approach that guides individuals toward a state of wholeness. It does this by integrating the realms of the mind, body, and spirit, helping individuals discover a more authentic, coherent, and harmonious state of being.

Engaging with the Mind

Somatic IFS begins with the mind, helping individuals recognize the multiplicity of their internal system—the various 'parts' or subpersonalities that influence their thoughts, feelings, and behaviors. By fostering a non-judgmental curiosity about these parts, Somatic IFS encourages individuals to develop an understanding and acceptance of all parts, ultimately leading to a more integrated mental state.

Consider a person who frequently experiences feelings of anxiety. Through Somatic IFS, they would learn to identify the part of them that carries this anxiety, understand its protective intentions, and develop a compassionate relationship with it.

Incorporating the Body

The "somatic" aspect of Somatic IFS brings the body into focus. By paying attention to body sensations, impulses, and tensions, individuals can gain further insights into their parts. This connection to the body allows for a more profound and embodied form of healing, integrating the physical with the psychological.

Continuing with the example above, the person struggling with anxiety might notice that their anxiety manifests as a tightness in their chest. By tuning into this bodily sensation and dialoguing with it as a part, they could facilitate a deeper level of healing and integration.

Cultivating the Self

Central to Somatic IFS is the concept of the Self—the spiritual core characterized by calmness, clarity, curiosity, compassion, and other qualities. By helping individuals access their Self and lead their internal system from this place, Somatic IFS fosters a sense of inner unity and coherence.

As the person in our example continues their work with Somatic IFS, they would learn to approach their anxiety and associated physical sensations from the standpoint of their Self. In doing so, they would foster a state of inner balance, integrating their mind, body, and spirit in the pursuit of wholeness.

Toward Wholeness

Wholeness in Somatic IFS is not about achieving a perfect state or eradicating parts that cause distress. Instead, it is about embracing all aspects of oneself—the good, the bad, the comfortable, the uncomfortable—and allowing them to coexist in harmony under the leadership of the Self. This holistic acceptance and integration of all parts can facilitate profound healing, personal growth, and a deep sense of inner peace.

Reflective Questions:

1. How do you perceive the concept of wholeness in the context of Somatic IFS?

2. How can you incorporate the principles of Somatic IFS in your journey towards wholeness?

3. How can engaging with your mind, body, and Self lead you towards a more integrated state of being?

Embodying the Self

Embodying the Self is a central goal of Somatic Internal Family Systems (IFS) Therapy. It refers to the practice of consistently accessing and operating from the Self, the spiritual core or essence of an individual, and manifesting its qualities in everyday life.

Accessing the Self

Accessing the Self begins with the recognition that the Self is not another part, but rather the seat of consciousness—an intrinsic, indomitable presence that exists within every individual. The Self is characterized by the "Eight Cs": Calmness, Curiosity, Clarity, Compassion, Confidence, Courage, Creativity, and Connectedness.

Somatic IFS Therapy encourages individuals to access their Self by creating space between the Self and the parts. This often involves asking parts to step back or unblend, thus allowing the Self to come forward. For instance, someone may ask their anxious part to relax and give space for the Self to lead the internal system.

Operating from the Self

Once the Self is accessed, the next step is learning to operate from this state—leading the internal system from the position of the Self. This involves communicating with the parts from the Self's perspective, which is non-judgmental, empathetic, and understanding.

A person might engage in a dialogue with their parts, asking them about their fears, concerns, and needs. They would approach this conversation with a sense of calm curiosity and open-hearted compassion, signaling to the parts that they are safe and valued.

Manifesting the Qualities of the Self

Embodying the Self is not just an internal process—it also involves manifesting the Self's qualities in everyday life. This can transform an individual's relationships, career, and overall outlook on life, bringing them in alignment with their authentic Self.

For example, a person operating from the Self might exhibit increased patience in their relationships, greater creativity in their work, and a deeper sense of connection with themselves and others. They may also demonstrate a remarkable resilience, able to navigate life's ups and downs with calmness and courage.

Embodying the Self: The Path to Wholeness

By accessing, operating from, and embodying the Self, individuals move toward a state of wholeness—a state of internal harmony where all parts are acknowledged and appreciated, and where the Self is in its rightful place as the leader of the internal system.

Reflective Questions:

1. How do you understand the concept of embodying the Self?

2. What steps can you take towards accessing and operating from your Self?

3. How can embodying the Self impact your journey
    towards wholeness and wellbeing?

Chapter 8: Conclusion – The Revolution in Psychotherapy

In this concluding chapter, we reflect on the powerful potential of Somatic Internal Family Systems (IFS) Therapy. We underscore its innovative contributions to psychotherapy and look towards the future of this groundbreaking approach.

The Revolution of Somatic IFS

Somatic IFS marks a significant evolution in the field of psychotherapy. By integrating the mind, body, and spirit, it takes a holistic approach towards healing that goes beyond conventional modalities. It opens up new avenues of self-exploration and self-understanding, helping individuals reconnect with their inner selves and navigate their journey towards wholeness.

The Somatic IFS approach empowers individuals, teaching them to become their own therapists. By fostering an understanding of their internal family system and providing tools to engage with their parts, Somatic IFS equips individuals with the skills to self-navigate their healing journey.

The Impact of Somatic IFS

The efficacy of Somatic IFS is evident in numerous case studies and testimonials. From anxiety and depression to trauma and addiction, Somatic IFS has shown promising results in treating a wide range of mental health conditions. Its applications extend beyond psychotherapy into personal growth, spiritual exploration, and conflict resolution.

Somatic IFS is not just a therapeutic approach—it's a path towards self-discovery, self-understanding, and ultimately, self-mastery. As more people discover and embrace this approach, it could lead to a profound shift in how society views and deals with mental health.

Looking Forward: The Future of Somatic IFS

As we take a moment to look beyond the present horizon and into the future of Somatic Internal Family Systems (IFS) Therapy, it's apparent that we're standing at the precipice of a new era in psychotherapy and mental health care.

Firstly, as research continues and our understanding deepens, Somatic IFS is likely to gain more acceptance and integration within mainstream therapy. Its success in treating various mental health conditions will continue to be documented, leading to increased confidence in its efficacy and a wider adoption among professionals in the field.

There are also several emerging areas of potential growth and development for Somatic IFS. With advancements in neuroscience and technology, our understanding of the mind-body connection will continue to expand, further validating the somatic approach. It's conceivable that future studies could provide more concrete physiological evidence supporting Somatic IFS, perhaps even uncovering new links between specific body sensations or movements and certain emotional states or parts.

Additionally, Somatic IFS's holistic approach aligns well with the increasing trend towards personalized medicine. As mental health care becomes more tailored to individual needs, Somatic IFS—with its emphasis on individual parts and personal narratives—could become an essential tool in creating personalized therapy plans.

The practice of Somatic IFS may also expand beyond the therapist's office. Its principles of self-awareness, self-compassion, and mindfulness are universal, and can be applied in a variety of contexts, including schools, workplaces, and even homes. As a self-help tool, it could empower individuals to take charge of their mental health, fostering a culture of self-care and wellbeing.

Lastly, the core values of Somatic IFS—the recognition of multiplicity, the practice of self-leadership, the honoring of each part's story, and the journey towards wholeness—could reshape societal norms and expectations. By fostering greater empathy, acceptance, and understanding, Somatic IFS holds the potential to create a ripple effect, leading to more compassionate communities and societies.

As we stand at the dawn of this new era, the promise of Somatic IFS is evident. As therapists, patients, researchers, and learners, we have the privilege of participating in this promising field. May we continue to explore, discover, and transform. The future of Somatic IFS shines brightly, and we are excited to journey with you into this brilliant new frontier.

Final Thoughts

As we close the pages on this exploration of Somatic Internal Family Systems Therapy, we find ourselves reflecting on the transformative journey this book has undertaken. From laying the foundational understanding of Internal Family Systems and Somatic Therapy to exploring the integrated approach of Somatic IFS, we have ventured into a dynamic, holistic perspective of mental health and wellbeing.

The goal of Somatic IFS, as we've understood it, isn't merely about symptom relief or problem-solving—it's about fostering a profound state of internal harmony, a wholeness that integrates mind, body, and spirit. It's about embracing the beautiful complexity of our internal world, recognizing our multitudes, and learning to lead our parts from the compassionate perspective of the Self.

The journey to wholeness is indeed a profound one—fraught with challenges, but also filled with discoveries, insights, and transformations. It is a journey of returning to our authentic selves, of reconnecting with our inherent wisdom, and of reclaiming our capacity for self-healing and self-growth.

The implications of Somatic IFS extend beyond the realm of psychotherapy. This approach offers a blueprint for self-awareness and self-leadership that can inform our relationships, our work, and our engagement with the world. It invites us to meet every aspect of our lives with curiosity, compassion, and courage, fundamentally altering the way we perceive ourselves and our place in the world.

Finally, let us remember that Somatic IFS isn't just a groundbreaking approach—it's an invitation. An invitation to understand ourselves better, to engage with our internal parts with empathy and respect, to embody our truest Self, and ultimately, to journey towards integration and wholeness.

Whether you are a therapist seeking to enrich your practice, or an individual on a journey of self-discovery, we hope this book has provided you with valuable insights, practical tools, and above all, a deep sense of possibility. May your journey with Somatic Internal Family Systems Therapy be as enriching, transformative, and groundbreaking as the therapy itself.

Reflective Questions:

1. What are your key takeaways from this book?

2. How will you apply the principles and techniques of Somatic IFS in your practice or personal life?

3. How do you envision the future of Somatic IFS and its impact on psychotherapy and beyond?

Resources and Further Reading

The following is a selection of resources, including books, articles, websites, and videos, for those interested in delving deeper into the subjects covered in this book.

Books

1. *Internal Family Systems Therapy* by Richard Schwartz – This is the definitive book on Internal Family Systems (IFS) Therapy by the founder of the approach itself.

2. *The Body Keeps the Score: Brain, Mind, and Body in the Healing of Trauma* by Bessel van der Kolk – An essential read on the impact of trauma on the body and the mind, and the role of somatic therapies in healing.

3. *Waking the Tiger: Healing Trauma* by Peter Levine – This book introduces Somatic Experiencing, a body-oriented approach to trauma.

4. *In An Unspoken Voice: How the Body Releases Trauma and Restores Goodness* by Peter Levine – Another seminal work by Peter Levine, exploring the silent language of the body.

Online Articles

5. <u>Introduction to the Internal Family Systems Model</u> – An overview of IFS by the IFS Institute.

6. <u>Understanding Somatic Therapy</u> – A comprehensive article on Psychology Today discussing the basics of Somatic Therapy.

Websites

7. <u>The IFS Institute</u> – The official website of the IFS Institute, providing a wealth of resources on IFS.

8. <u>The Somatic Experiencing Trauma Institute</u> – The official website of the Somatic Experiencing Trauma Institute, offering resources on Somatic Experiencing and trauma recovery.

Videos

9. <u>Dr. Richard Schwartz: Introduction to the Internal Family Systems Model</u> – A lecture by Dr. Richard Schwartz, introducing the Internal Family Systems model.

10. <u>Healing Trauma: Restoring the Wisdom of the Body – Peter Levine</u> – A lecture by Peter Levine, discussing Somatic Experiencing and trauma recovery.

This list is by no means exhaustive, but it provides a starting point for further exploration into the fascinating world of Somatic Internal Family Systems Therapy. Happy reading!

www.ingramcontent.com/pod-product-compliance
Lightning Source LLC
Chambersburg PA
CBHW050034260726
48658CB00005B/1604